THE TIME IS NOW

Take Action and Create the Life You Desire

AN INSPIRATIONAL **GRATITUDE** DOT JOURNAL
FOR BUSY WOMEN ON THE GO

Paulette Bonneur

This journal belongs to

....
....
....
....

Introduction

Are you ready to get to work? I am going to assume since you purchased this journal the answer to that is yes!

When was the last time you took a moment to just breathe? To reflect on your life and what you are most grateful for? The things that make your heart smile and propel you forward? If it has been a while, it's okay.

The purpose of this journal is to prompt you to write down and keep track of the things in your life that you are most grateful for, recognize what you already have, and take action.

Let's face it; as a woman time can sometimes be a scarce resource. This dot journal was created with busy schedules in mind. Thought provoking quick writing that is similar to traditional journaling but in a fraction of the time. Keep it by your bedside, in your purse, backpack, gym bag, take it on a flight, use it during the workday, or write during a quick escape.

Wherever you are, take advantage of the opportunity to write your thoughts down. This journal will help you identify threads of gratitude throughout your day while encouraging you to think about actionable steps you can take to create the life you want.

Many studies, articles, and publications note a plethora of benefits directly related to journaling. Some of which include: reduce anxiety and depression, memory function improvement, stress reduction, and so much more.

Combined with the benefits of practicing gratitude such as increased mood, resilience, and other positive outcomes, this journal is the perfect start to living a better life. Remember, consistency is key so try to write in your journal daily or as often as possible.

Focus

Since so much time is spent at work, with family, and attempting to do a million things throughout the day it can be easy to lose sight of what is most important... YOU!

In order to help you take time each day to focus on what matters most, this journal consists of many prompts.

Take notice of even the smallest things that deserve gratitude and take action in the direction of your dreams with a grateful heart.

By setting aside some time each day to focus on gratitude journaling, you have the ability to shift your vibration and create the life you desire.

The time is now, go after what you want and acknowledge and recognize what you already have.

Gratitude

Let's keep your first challenge simple. Write down one thing you are grateful for every day for a month. This is a simple way to help you establish a habit of gratitude.

1

2

3

4

5

6

7

8

9

10

11

12

13

14

15

16

17

18

19

20

21

22

23

24

25

26

27

28

29

30

31

It's very common to notice some changes in your life once you've start practicing daily gratitude. After your first month of journaling you may sleep better, experience less stress, or feel more satisfied in all areas of your life.

Perhaps these changes will make you eager to see what deeper exploration of gratitude may bring. If this is the case, feel free to jump ahead to the prompted section of this journal. There are over 50 prompts to help you get started. Kudos for doing the work and taking the first step. Let's get into it!

Daily Gratitude

I woke up feeling...

3 Things I am grateful for...

My affirmation of the day...

A role model I am grateful for ...

My action item for tomorrow...

I am ending the day feeling...

Daily Gratitude

Date: _____

I woke up feeling...

3 Things I am grateful for...

My affirmation of the day...

A recent compliment that meant a lot to me ..

My action item for tomorrow...

I am ending the day feeling...

Daily Gratitude

I woke up feeling...

3 Things I am grateful for...

My affirmation of the day...

Someone in my life I am grateful for ...

My action item for tomorrow...

I am ending the day feeling...

Daily Gratitude

Date: _____

I woke up feeling...

3 Things I am grateful for...

My affirmation of the day...

Ways in which I show my gratitude ...

My action item for tomorrow...

I am ending the day feeling...

Daily Gratitude

Date:

I woke up feeling...

3 Things I am grateful for...

My affirmation of the day...

People who mean the most to me...

My action item for tomorrow...

I am ending the day feeling...

Daily Gratitude

I woke up feeling...

3 Things I am grateful for...

My affirmation of the day...

My guilty pleasure ...

My action item for tomorrow...

I am ending the day feeling...

Daily Gratitude

Date: _____

I woke up feeling...

3 Things I am grateful for...

My affirmation of the day...

An opportunity I am grateful for ...

My action item for tomorrow...

I am ending the day feeling...

Daily Gratitude

Date: _____

I woke up feeling...

3 Things I am grateful for...

My affirmation of the day...

My favorite wind down activity ...

My action item for tomorrow...

I am ending the day feeling...

Daily Gratitude

I woke up feeling...

3 Things I am grateful for...

My affirmation of the day...

A quote that uplifts me ...

My action item for tomorrow...

I am ending the day feeling...

Daily Gratitude

Date: _____

I woke up feeling...

3 Things I am grateful for...

My affirmation of the day...

A future event I am excited about ...

My action item for tomorrow...

I am ending the day feeling...

Daily Gratitude

Date: _____

I woke up feeling...

3 Things I am grateful for...

My affirmation of the day...

My favorite place to go ...

My action item for tomorrow...

I am ending the day feeling...

Daily Gratitude

I woke up feeling...

3 Things I am grateful for...

My affirmation of the day...

A talent I am grateful for...

My action item for tomorrow...

I am ending the day feeling...

Daily Gratitude

Date: _____

I woke up feeling...

3 Things I am grateful for...

My affirmation of the day...

Something that has changed for the better ...

My action item for tomorrow...

I am ending the day feeling...

Daily Gratitude

Date: _____

I woke up feeling...

3 Things I am grateful for...

My affirmation of the day...

Someone who helped me get through a difficult time...

My action item for tomorrow...

I am ending the day feeling...

Daily Gratitude

Date: _____

I woke up feeling...

3 Things I am grateful for...

My affirmation of the day...

Action I took towards reaching my goals ...

My action item for tomorrow...

I am ending the day feeling...

Daily Gratitude

I woke up feeling...

3 Things I am grateful for...

My affirmation of the day...

Something I take comfort in ...

My action item for tomorrow...

I am ending the day feeling...

Daily Gratitude

Date: _____

I woke up feeling...

3 Things I am grateful for...

My affirmation of the day...

A modern convenience I appreciate...

My action item for tomorrow...

I am ending the day feeling...

Daily Gratitude

Date: _____

I woke up feeling...

3 Things I am grateful for...

My affirmation of the day...

A hidden blessing in a difficult situation...

My action item for tomorrow...

I am ending the day feeling...

Daily Gratitude

I woke up feeling...

3 Things I am grateful for...

My affirmation of the day...

My favorite song lyric ...

My action item for tomorrow...

I am ending the day feeling...

Daily Gratitude

Date: _____

I woke up feeling...

3 Things I am grateful for...

My affirmation of the day...

Something beautiful I recently observed ...

My action item for tomorrow...

I am ending the day feeling...

Daily Gratitude

I woke up feeling...

3 Things I am grateful for...

My affirmation of the day...

Something that made me smile today ...

My action item for tomorrow...

I am ending the day feeling...

Daily Gratitude

I woke up feeling...

3 Things I am grateful for...

My affirmation of the day...

My proudest accomplishment...

My action item for tomorrow...

I am ending the day feeling...

Daily Gratitude

Date: _____

I woke up feeling...

3 Things I am grateful for...

My affirmation of the day...

Something good that happened today....

My action item for tomorrow...

I am ending the day feeling...

Daily Gratitude

Date: _____

I woke up feeling...

3 Things I am grateful for...

My affirmation of the day...

A book I would recommend to a friend ...

My action item for tomorrow...

I am ending the day feeling...

Daily Gratitude

I woke up feeling...

3 Things I am grateful for...

My affirmation of the day...

A memory that makes me smile ...

My action item for tomorrow...

I am ending the day feeling...

Daily Gratitude

Date: _____

I woke up feeling...

3 Things I am grateful for...

My affirmation of the day...

Something I like at the moment ...

My action item for tomorrow...

I am ending the day feeling...

Daily Gratitude

Date:

I woke up feeling...

3 Things I am grateful for...

My affirmation of the day...

My favorite season ...

My action item for tomorrow...

I am ending the day feeling...

Daily Gratitude

Date:

I woke up feeling...

3 Things I am grateful for...

My affirmation of the day...

An accomplishment I am proud of...

My action item for tomorrow...

I am ending the day feeling...

Daily Gratitude

Date: _____

I woke up feeling...

3 Things I am grateful for...

My affirmation of the day...

The biggest gift in my life right now...

My action item for tomorrow...

I am ending the day feeling...

Daily Gratitude

Date: _____

I woke up feeling...

3 Things I am grateful for...

My affirmation of the day...

Someone who has had an impact on my life...

My action item for tomorrow...

I am ending the day feeling...

Daily Gratitude

I woke up feeling...

3 Things I am grateful for...

My affirmation of the day...

A challenge I am grateful for...

My action item for tomorrow...

I am ending the day feeling...

Daily Gratitude

Date: _____

I woke up feeling...

3 Things I am grateful for...

My affirmation of the day...

My favorite thing to do outside...

My action item for tomorrow...

I am ending the day feeling...

Daily Gratitude

I woke up feeling...

3 Things I am grateful for...

My affirmation of the day...

The best part of my day...

My action item for tomorrow...

I am ending the day feeling...

Daily Gratitude

Date: _____

I woke up feeling...

3 Things I am grateful for...

My affirmation of the day...

Good news I received recently ...

My action item for tomorrow...

I am ending the day feeling...

Daily Gratitude

Date: _____

I woke up feeling...

3 Things I am grateful for...

My affirmation of the day...

Something I plan to take action towards ...

My action item for tomorrow...

I am ending the day feeling...

Daily Gratitude

Date: _____

I woke up feeling...

3 Things I am grateful for...

My affirmation of the day...

The best gift I've ever received ...

My action item for tomorrow...

I am ending the day feeling...

Daily Gratitude

Date: _____

I woke up feeling...

3 Things I am grateful for...

My affirmation of the day...

The item I cherish the most...

My action item for tomorrow...

I am ending the day feeling...

Daily Gratitude

Date: ———

I woke up feeling...

3 Things I am grateful for...

My affirmation of the day...

A trait of mine I am grateful for ...

My action item for tomorrow...

I am ending the day feeling...

Daily Gratitude

Date: _____

I woke up feeling...

3 Things I am grateful for...

My affirmation of the day...

Things that bring me joy...

My action item for tomorrow...

I am ending the day feeling...

Daily Gratitude

I woke up feeling...

3 Things I am grateful for...

My affirmation of the day...

My favorite thing to do with family ...

My action item for tomorrow...

I am ending the day feeling...

Daily Gratitude

Date: _____

I woke up feeling...

3 Things I am grateful for...

My affirmation of the day...

One thing I love about myself ...

My action item for tomorrow...

I am ending the day feeling...

Daily Gratitude

I woke up feeling...

3 Things I am grateful for...

My affirmation of the day...

What I love most about being a woman...

My action item for tomorrow...

I am ending the day feeling...

Daily Gratitude

Date: _____

I woke up feeling...

3 Things I am grateful for...

My affirmation of the day...

Something kind I did today ...

My action item for tomorrow...

I am ending the day feeling...

Daily Gratitude

Date: _____

I woke up feeling...

3 Things I am grateful for...

3 things you are grateful for...

The most exciting place I've traveled to ...

My action item for tomorrow...

I am ending the day feeling...

Daily Gratitude

I woke up feeling...

3 Things I am grateful for...

My affirmation of the day...

Something that makes me feel confident...

My action item for tomorrow...

I am ending the day feeling...

Daily Gratitude

Date: _____

I woke up feeling...

3 Things I am grateful for...

My affirmation of the day...

What I love about my body...

My action item for tomorrow...

I am ending the day feeling...

Daily Gratitude

Date: _____

I woke up feeling...

3 Things I am grateful for...

My affirmation of the day...

On the weekend I love to ...

My action item for tomorrow...

I am ending the day feeling...

Daily Gratitude

I woke up feeling...

3 Things I am grateful for...

My affirmation of the day...

A past lesson I am grateful for ...

My action item for tomorrow...

I am ending the day feeling...

Daily Gratitude

Date: _____

I woke up feeling...

3 Things I am grateful for...

My affirmation of the day...

A rejection I am grateful for (now)...

My action item for tomorrow...

I am ending the day feeling...

Daily Gratitude

Date: _____

I woke up feeling...

3 Things I am grateful for...

My affirmation of the day...

My favorite thing about nature ...

My action item for tomorrow...

I am ending the day feeling...

Reflection

What a journey! You did the work now it is time to think about what this experience has taught you. Jot down a few thoughts as you reflect on your writing throughout this journal.

Notes

Notes

Notes

Notes

Notes

Notes

Notes

Notes

Notes

Notes

Made in the USA
Monee, IL
07 October 2023

44087900R00072